For Dave & Greta —

who neighboured

the

THE BOOK OF CONTRADICTIONS

and have enjoyed
the ritual "irrigations"
and mutual confusions

from

George
November
2002

The Book of
Contradictions

George McWhirter

OOLICHAN BOOKS
LANTZVILLE, BRITISH COLUMBIA, CANADA
2002

National Library of Canada Cataloguing in Publication Data

McWhirter, George.
    The book of contradictions

    Poems.
    ISBN 0-88982-206-9

    I. Title.
PS8575.W48B66 2002   C811'.54   C2002-910110-7
PR9199.3.M3415B66 2002

The Canada Council | Le Conseil des Arts
    for the Arts | du Canada

We gratefully acknowledge the support of the Canada Council for the Arts for our publishing program.

BRITISH
COLUMBIA
ARTS COUNCIL
Supported by the Province of British Columbia

Grateful acknowledgement is also made to the BC Ministry of Tourism, Small Business and Culture for their financial support.

We acknowledge the financial support of the Government of Canada through the Book Publishing Industry Development Program for our publishing activities.

Published by
Oolichan Books
P.O. Box 10, Lantzville
British Columbia, Canada
V0R 2H0

Printed in Canada

Acknowledgements

Poems from this book have appeared in *BC Studies*, *The Harvard Review*, *London Magazine*, *Mantis*, *Poetry Canada Review*, *Quarry*, *Stand*, *The Phoenix Review*. Some were anthologized in *Inside The Poem*, edited by W.H. New, Oxford University Press, *Witness To Wilderness (The Clayoquot Sound Anthology)* edited by Howard Breen-Needham, Sandy Frances Duncan, Deborah Ferens, Phyllis Reeve and Susan Yates, Arsenal Pulp Press.

The poems—"A Woman of Ireland," "Sunday Is the Lord's Day Off," "Memoir," "In the River the Sap of the World Flows Out of All Its Tributaries," "Uncle Dick and the Butterflies," "1941," "Fab," "Ali Baba & the Forty Thousand Bees," and "For Angela"—were published in the chapbook, *FAB*, by the Hawthorne Society, Victoria, 1997. As the winner of its Canadian Chapbook Competition, "Ovid in Saskatchewan" was published by League of Canadian Poets in May 1998. The set of poems after "A Warning on the Subject Matter of This Poem" in Section II *(Kindling)* was a finalist in the CBC Literary Competition.

The author is grateful for the use of the image "Rainbow Room" by Abel Quezada.

CONTENTS

¡ A WORD ON THE BILLBOARDS OF AMERICA!

Why is North American poetry so flat, prosy and slow? The prairie running through the middle of it all. It's those distances between. By the time folk reach their neighbour, they have half-forgotten how to talk, and the few words they pick out are filled with the wonder of the things between. This way they use a little to cover a lot. It might be a magical economy of words, but one can never quite remember those words, only the things behind them. It is the words that are forgettable, not the places. This isn't so of billboards. Faced with an ad line from a billboard and a line of verse—say, plastered against a landscape, how many remember the billboard's line and forget the verse, though the intent and nature of the verse is as noble as its subject?

And the lines on those islands as tight and tidy as their fields. Around rock and drumlin, they twist, the arterial roads that arc around henges and arch over heath. At Slieve bottom, they stop to browse on whin and heather, their backs to the sea: flat, black sheep, severed from the free fold on the slope. Like the ink of words from the wild, they keep to themselves.

Which do I call home, the wide acres of wheat and the sabre tooth of the Rockies or blue humpback Slieve, its mangers and pens of meaning? The same snow white bleat from their corries leads in this ocular music, a decibel too pure for string and fret, or flute, in any stanza of mine.

\

For Angela

This is the origin of asthma:
a woman

planted in a garden
of her own perfume

in our living room.
This is the other origin of asthma:
the damp roads,
my father volunteered for

in 1914,

the retreats
cobbled

with the carcasses of horses,
the mud

ribbed with stallions
where the rain races over the stones

into an anonymity of brown,
where the eyes

like drops of water
settle into a sea of matter.

This is the origin of asthma
I flee

in all my choking.
Not the killing or the carnage:

but being alive in this,
the eye wells

filling up
with the brown blink of mud

that boots tramp in.
There lies the origin of asthma

in my father's memory
the muddled echo

in the furrow of my choking at the
other end of the century,

these affectionate anxieties
I hate to breathe in—

like feathers
off a dove

that stop the sky
I had in my lungs

where I climbed

under my mother's skirts to hide
from my father's stories

and there eating into
her flesh,

holding up
her battered nylons,

I recognise

the elastic band
from my catapult

that brings down

all these birds
which flutter

in my throat and chest
forever—

the lace of women's underwear.
Here is the origin of asthma—

breathing in and in
without being able
to breathe out

a word of it,
this love

that encumbers
and rules over me

like the queen's pavilion
in the field

killing me with canopy
and canapé,

trampled hay and humidity,

this moody
falcon,

thick with spit
on straw and feather

that has caught up with me
in the air.

Here is the origin of asthma:
this whistling in my chest,

that calls the dog
and terrifies the wife

docking the stamen
on the rhododendron,

ordering the soil
to give her back
what she wants,

her father,
dead of emphysema
when she was eleven,

history repeating
itself through the living
when I kiss

with the rasp
of grass in my throat.

This dandelion
down, this lawn is the origin

of asthma, all this mangled army
of organs and feelings

in my chest,

this murdered
and murdering matter

that clogs the voices
underground

that want her to hear them
say,

we would fill the earth

over and over
with our dying
just to lie here at your feet.

A WOMAN OF IRELAND

On the road home I saw a woman
with a pram full of nettles
and a milk bottle in it to calm
the prickling rancour,
perhaps, that grew around the child
she had left on whose doorstep.

Her hands appeared to me
larger than any human's for holding
what was no longer there.
Those breasts of hers would feed
only the bog, and her breath—
the grey fog, growing out of the sea.
What words could I lend to her story,
coming home, much better off
than when I went away?

'Bless the big cars,' she sighs by the roadside,
'for they have the money that makes no mistake.
When I couldn't name what I owned
I delivered a piece of my own body
to their doorstep
and they took it in.

'What's wrong with me?
I asked only for a son's ring
on my finger and would have worn it
through the nose. The sun
goes down as red as a Sunday roast.

'If one can live off the road
with this little, two
could have done twice as well:
one holding a basket
while the other filled it
from the hedge.

'Birds, your legs are a skinny disgrace.
No wonder you are always flying
away from them'.

Home, I can hear her pram
bumping over the stones
in the stream, and 'There,
there,' she still says to her bottle
as if it were my face
sleeping among the nettles.

A LITTLE SOMETHING IN THE MAIL
ABOUT ELECTION TIME

If Harry and Hilda Smith should wake up one day
with a great idea about changing the political map
of the world, Harry or Hilda (whoever rises first
to put it into effect) should be placed on a small island
in a large lake of cold water, but every ordinary
comfort available at hand.
Now, in order to deliver their idea to any other soul
beyond the immediate family, Harry or Hilda
must swim across to the nearest telephone
booth, there to find instead of any telephonic device—
pen, envelope and paper. The glue for the stamp
must be very clearly poisoned and kept
where there is no other source of moisture bar
the tongue's.

All this, of course, is an improvisation on the messenger myth.

If Harry or Hilda Smith can bring his or her self to give their idea
the last lick of conviction, the sender of the good news
dies.

If Harry or Hilda can persuade any other Hilda
or Harry to lick and mail it, the original Harry or Hilda will have
committed murder and suffer the full consequence of the law
for their persuasion.

This is how we must address all our good ideas.

WHATEVER IT IS YOU MUST EAT IT

Which is it to be?

Ideals
or meals.

What if the ideal
is a meal?

What shall we do then

with all the fresh ideas
in our new republic?

A RED COAT FOR A LADY

Scarlet drips of paint
on the grey concrete step
thrill me
as if Snow White's
lips had fallen
at my feet.

I touch the curdled kiss
from the pot I carried
to the raw wood
of our bedroom chair.

If paint could feel,
would it miss
the touch of your hips
more than me
before you went to sleep?

No kiss of mine
can revive
the freshness
of that finish

Ages pass and the red gloss
needs reviving
with a lick or two of paint.

In the garage
I steep my stick
in the rusty can
where a thick skin

has grown over
the toxic colour

like a second lover.

In our garden,
an apple

or the sun rattles
in a throat of leaves

and summer,
which was lodged there,

choking
on the cobwebs, gurgles

out of a well
in the broken skin of the pot:

a rude
red word,

as if the passion
clotted in your heart

came up through your mouth
and fell like blood

on the bare steps.
The chair too

is dying
for the stick and brush

with which I painted the rare
embrace

that stirs you
from this dull legend of sleep.

FAB

There was an island and there was a wind.
Women spread their washing on the hedges

And on the thorn tree that could not grow
Above a few feet.

The white clouds in the sky
Mocked the Sunday shirts.

Like wrists and hands out of the cuffs
The birds rose and twisted in their flight.

Summer settled precariously;
Winter lived off nothing at all:

Rock and rosaries. Before central heating,
The people put on more clothes to bed

Than Forty-coats, the beggar.

Bundles of green bushes
Waited bereft

When electric dryers
Were put in, and women walked by

Those naked foundlings,
Thinking of pence,

Less for the collection plate,
More for the parking meter, the coke machine.

Isn't it the age of automation, they thought.
They remembered their grandparents

Plucking sheets and shirts
That had rips and tears in them

As if the twigs and thorns knew all along
That their green machinery

Was no good, only useful
To put linen

Up for inspection, once upon a time,
To Heaven

While they still believed in that.
Long johns and liberty vests

Poked with a stick through the first
Skin-scalding detergents: Fab

Tide in the old
Omnipotent outdoors.

ALI BABA & THE FORTY THOUSAND BEES

1.

The snails are sailing like whales in the wet.
I remember in a warmer time,
a ball of ice cream, still frigid
from the freezer, slid out of the scoop
and slammed into some tomatoes in a bowl.

Across the garden, later, I
dropped a lump of damaged banana
for the dog. It bounced off her nose
onto a bumble bee. In the grass,
our bitch gobbled them both—the furry-
legged *hors d'oeuvres* coated
in banana slick. The buzz of those black
and yellow sweetnesses stung her mouth.

She looked around, turned; looked
around, turned—as if a button
had been pressed to point her
snapping at the next slippery
hum that came up behind her—
that nipped her taste for bananas
in the bud.

2.
I see you bend into the raspberries.
I lunge, indecently, with the wish
to kiss you there where you have oft
sautéed my tongue in butter and brine,
but the slime and soft dirt
under my heel pitch and toss
me onto my spine. My hands hit
concrete first, and throb

as though they had arrived
at their destination and caught
the treasure of your haunches
burning like the hive of forty
thousand bees in the bush.

LAST FIRS

Like silly wooden
watches hidden in the soil
digging over our vegetable plot
I come upon the filberts the gluey
kernels of the summer hours hardened in
side where they are pocketed in loam After
a drop by the diligent and delinquent crows they
knock on the fence posts or the stones or the paved
path but missing anything hard enough or when
the stellar's jays or the crows chip at them on the metal
cap atop the telegraph pole they skyte off
as if in a game of equally silly billiards and are
sunk in the last grass cuttings for the compost bin
For weeks the back lanes have been bombed with
damsons like the fat blue tongues of the gods
spat down from the thunderclouds
their bruised black prophesies
made ready to be reborn
transplanted
into plum trees

Armageddonish
a haze laces the air smoke
and ash from the subdivision
where the developers and builders
open the earth
for the airborne packagers of orchards

their battering out
the next meal
becomes forgivable greed
if it does devolution's work

no more dinosaurish
conifers at road's end
rash-inviting needlework
in the cedars
a deciduous *arrondissement*
instead
after the big banging
of heavy machinery
and the burnings when
the nuts wake
in their own fine accidental
time the sweet plans of Eden
revised
sunk home through the prickling
the sweating and the cursing
by the likes of me
whose flailing
spade turns them in again too deeply to reveal

HOW SINGULAR YOU ARE

Overtures of slender
blue
asparagus,

the light
counts them all
as one.

Only the pear tree,
bowed low
with the numbers
on its branches,

understands
each ripe
subtraction
the wind makes.

We are suspended
on the thin
thread of an equation,

the transparently
easy

mathematics of the morning light:
freshly-invented

mushroom,
the zero of the sun

about which
we are a plus.

Tapered cylinders
of asparagus,

these organ
pipes

from whose
top flukes

blossom
the curled green

ears for the dominant chord
in the soil.

Fibred
with the square root

of raw reason
you and I

are not sure
of this instinct

for a sovereign
indivisible sky.

ON PANCAKE EATING
AT THE FEAST OF ST. JOHN

1.

We all turn to sugar, paradoxically,
In the cap, where we have been twisted
Hard, screwed on with a snap
By our mother or our father to keep
Our love in, fresh, like the maple syrup—

As if mouths loosened with greed,
Lips as curdled as the molten
Pancake batter across the bevelled
Skillet, drooling all around us,
Could coax it out of the bottle.

But once love is gone, and this is all
That's left—a brown rust stuck
Around the rim, I am driven
Back to lick the place
Where sweetness scabbed the glass.

2.

When we walked in the wood, it was June;
The salmonberry leaves were green,
Their stalks slender
And ginger, the berries like
Jewelled upside-down temples
Raised to become solid vessels
For the light. They filled
With the dark worship of the ground—
This prickly vermouth in our mouths

Vinted from the sour
Sap of the salmonberries through
The lanky spigots rooted there.

I offered you six or seven,
A handful of plump prayers,
Hoping you would look at me
And forgive, confer no more
With the conifers about my weaknesses.

I plucked one for myself and bit
Into a whitened worm inside
And wondered why we could not always
Savour our decay, eat into the corruption
Where it has supped and gone granular
To become the roughest, dearest
Sugar of the fruit?

PSALM

We have grown old
and ripe,

truffled and
underworldly,

as pampered with the damp
and precarious

as a tuft
of moss,

kicked like a toupee
off the curb-side

where we clung
growling

like velvet green
terriers

dislodged
by a jogger's heel

or toe.
Haven't you seen them

like the church-goers
of a Sunday,

spilling
immortally

across the road,
defying any traffic

other than
what passes

between them
and their godliness?

This piety
pelts by

like the heaven-ripened
rain

past the slow
immaculate assumption

of a dog turd
by the slug.

Dead slow
and sweet,

from the same still,
the drip

that lays the dew.
Are these souls

too good to rot
and enter

a green and brown
bargain

with their maker
and the ground?

What quickens best?
The rain,

the perspiration
of creation.

The world does laps
at 0 – 1000 miles per hour.

Lie down in it a bit
Was the earth not made

to do this racing
round for you.

SUNDAY IS THE LORD'S DAY OFF

Those long brown silences
across the ploughed fields,
Those shoes put by the door
To make it easier
To step out when we set
Our feet inside
The polished leather of
A Sunday, so he could feel
Them and walk
More lordly or loudly.
They blessed him
with their strange
pain and awkwardness.
The Prince of Peace, almost
Vanished from our later
Prosperity, was made
To walk as unused
As we on slippery soles,
But grateful that we had let
Him get a toe in.

There were those
Who thought of him
Between satin sheets,
No less difficult for him
To accommodate—the benediction
Of that swaddling
So bodiless, and the appetite
Put too much into its
Adornment, the
Cup and its design of flowers,
Not the coffee.

When they slipped
Into the bath with him,
He was sorry if the salts
And porcelain could not make
Him sneeze. He fizzed
For them dutifully.
The water—washing
His own feet,
The tiredness draining
From them, rising
In a creamy skim
Like fat.

Hard to tell them apart
Luxuries of laziness
Or the truly
Tired. That is why
There were always the blue
Bath salts and the brown
Stain of the field,
To keep up appearances
In the toilet.

Like water on the face
Or feet—his omniscience
Did not discriminate
Between high and low.

He asked each to enter
His or her mark,
Then saw which truly
Deserved to be their own,
And which he should wash
Out of mind.

If necessary
He can remember
To the hundred thousandth
Dilution how our bodies
Served his pleasure
In passing.

MEMOIR

Does this groiny-loin or high-cut of the new
Swim suits that makes the women's legs
Look like chicken or turkey
Drumsticks, which my eyes gnaw on
Till they're bored and sore,
Upset me? Is there too much easy
Protein, too much battery
Breeding in this beauty? Am I
Too much a longer-after
The monogamy of parrots whose sex
I will never see for feathers, like my gaunt
Grandmother, taller in her flowered smock
Than my grandfather: a sailor, who brought
her this talking bird he'd taught to hiss
A *double entendre*: "Alas, a lass,"
They synchronised the sibilants
As he sat mated to that female word
Who shed her whole body. Like my grandmother
When she finally took off, her legs
Reached up to heaven in one transcendental
Flutter, leaving grandfather with a
Hole in his vocabulary.

Would he be shocked to spy
A lycra-strangled lass, her crotch
Bulging at him like a plastic eye-patch?
Or would he prefer to catch them
In something as innocuous as socks
And sneakers, or long culottes when the women
Slip into loose summer gear and his only
Observation could be, "Cool",
And not "all ass", the way "Ah, lass"
Would sound in his rough mid-Ulster
Accent as the girls float
Out of their dressing rooms to stand
Plumed—not plucked, by the edge of the silver sea,
Like capons on a platter, fit only
For the greasy gluttony
Of king or commoner.

But now *this triple-entendre* keeps flying like a rebel
Tricolour at half-mast or winging
Through my head—"Alas a lass all ass."
Was that the friendly
Feathered-reminder to my grandmother
From that sailor, who came in
With coal off a collier and this repetitive present
Of a parrot for his pregnant lass
Who he had stripped once and left
Tied to their tongues in Glenarm,
Broiling under the eyes of every gossip
With those long legs in the air.

IN THE RIVER, THE SAP OF THE WORLD FLOWS OUT OF ALL ITS TRIBUTARIES

I never could play the scales on the piano well,
but in my youth I was a climber.
There were always leaves around my face,
a veil of twigs that made believe
I was lovely, or not there
at all in any visible way,
composed of the common camouflage
that the trees by every field
provided, like I could
have been a mobile apple
in their branches, or
a plum, or all pumped up with pap,
as prickly green in the corrusc
as the horse chestnut,
but I could not suffer
the come down
to earth. If truth
be known I still re-dream
my fear at being so indeterminate.
In the night, when the wind raises
its airy anthem
in the trees, too wild
to sleep beside you, I wear the bark again
and grunting in my throat
for the hairy hymn I make
at the fork of your limbs.

DECEMBER WEDDING

She looked out
        the landscape bare its music
escaped into the air
remembered kisses
        and the grey growling of the tide
plump stones
        that slithered over each other
like pups
        (no matter
which way they turn
        each
believes the other
        blocks a teat)
kisses

        or misses They were
the top of the tree
        leaves
listening
        for every nuance on the wind
the ripeness of the rope
        growing
from the hanged-man's
        throat

They drove over the Queen's Bridge,
                then
heading for deep South Down
                along the Newtownards Road
past where they made the stays at the Ropeworks
                The workers could walk a while and see it
the rough
                fruit of their toil at the Queen's Quay
mooring a tanker
                to a bollard
the tug of fertility
                full commerce in the hank

They drove on to Newtownards
                then to Comber
What had they been
                a-wooing of—
the rope of wedlock?

                Perhaps in the worn
strand's hempen blur
                they saw
the downy forearm of a fiancée
                across her young man's shoulder
her hand
                at the nape of the neck
arranging as if it were
                a target at a fair
or a manikin
                whose expression
must come to its only life
                in the magic window of her touch

The mirror of that morning held
a horror travelling through summer
the dust in the lane falls
behind a Jaguar

like the powder on her face
as she looks into the glass suddenly

as leery as a driver into the rear view
mirror of the car that has just crushed
a cat

The bones of the afternoon
are pale and white
picked-through
Or is she simply tender
at the tragedy of her permanent arrival
in his house
stooping to miss the headstone of his forebears
at the door?

But going home to her own childhood haunts her
                    Steam from its engine
history
                    the coarse belch of its chimney
always fell
                    on wild strawberries
fertilised by the ash
                    of a last year's fire that blazed
along the whole embankment
                    and made of the stray engine sparks
a flock of hissing birds
                    passing on the train the faces of her family
at the window bubble
                    white as potatoes in a pot

They lay where they lay
by the Belfast Co. Down Railway
her breasts flattened against him
two pennies on a rail
Doubt is the doorstop
winter kisses bring in a spring
through the open door
and they made if not love
its coefficient

The wind in her ear
                    is off the Irish Sea
the one in his
                    off Slieve Binyan

Whose fear rises higher
                    in the morning?

He pants
                    because he races from the cold in her
She is cold
                    because she fears the slavery
her fixing
                    a hot meal for the rest of her life

The dishes are as done as they always will be
                    There is an electric stove
in the galley of a kitchen
                    The mountain
and its wall behind the house
                    are mourning her arrival
adding the hardness of her heart
                    to the pile
the wildness of her temper
                    to the wind's

                    Vaguely she watches him
                    rise

                    boat unable
                    to climb the hill of the horizon

"I've played him enough rope" she says

as he turns anchored
in the twists of sheet

mouth yawing
toward breakfast off her teats

but still she lies stroking the hair
on his arm as if it were the ship's cat

and the stomach full of kittens
it has given her

she will never be able to drown

Though the bucket
in the shaft
sinks deeper than the sea

though the rope
that holds the bucket
is longer
than their love

her heart breaks
with all the weight of water

in its well

UNCLE DICK & THE BUTTERFLIES

I

"Tell me if they're out flying, like pages
cut from the Book of Kells, and I'll come too,"

Said Uncle Dick, his expression as regular
As the green convolvulus of summer

About his butterflies. Out flying
In all their embroidery,

The peaks on their wings
As big and flat as his ears, clapped

To the sheerness of Japanese screens
In his sailor's days, where the kimonos

He remembered collapsed with a thud of cloth,
And the women walked

In their bare skin, as fat and fleshily as tulip
Petals all about the boulders and round rocks.

The bulged thumbs and heels of his hands
Parted to let one go, the Monarch of his

Soul, gaoled for a moment in a gesture,
Yet no dust of theirs

Smudged his fingers—so immaculate
A raconteur was my Uncle Dick.

II
They were the yellows
And the browns of all the wasps

And female testiness he had ever known,
Pressed

Into a silence of perfection, a resurrection
Like the morning, on wings as wicked fine

As the Gillette razor blades he shaved with, cleaned
And dried. For slitting dragons' throats,
He told us, the ones he brooded on in the margins
To the Book of Kells, where capital letters crawled

With creatures and creations, in a text of verses
He had followed all his life, though he could

Not read the Latin in the *Song of Solomon* displayed
And had not seen it till that day-trip

Down to Dublin. But still the pages separated and book-
Ended him each summer in the lane, by the bugled

Convolvulus that learns its lesson off of any column
Or upright whatsoever, and speaks the same language

As the roses or the Romans. He wandered around
The words of love hung in the many-roomed

Volume: Monarchs
In an art gallery of the air,

Their bodies no bigger than a hinge
Between two abstract paintings—

The butterflies & the Book of Kells.
The meanings coloured round those lines

Opened at him like his lifetime cravings
In a glass case. A library of angels and double,

Paper-panelled doors
In a house, drawn-wide

To let them in—drafts of white, white women
With black, black hair. Letters

In a literature of lovely ideographs.
With his creased trousers, Uncle Dick

Creaked out of the shadows
Into the sun. Such straight and simple lines.

Age made him almost orientally slow
And jerky as their flight. Like sampan sails

They rocked, climbing in tiers;
On wings as brittle as bamboo and lacquered

Paper sails, they crept up to the high
Horizon of his vision until he could not tell if he had

Sailed into THE BIBLE, or our garden, when he came
Hoving in from Dublin, confirming that it was warm,

Summer's zenith in their dance and at the numbered
Page top which he leaned down to see his face in,

Swimming with the Saints
And Scholars at Trinity College. Now, for me

The mould and the maggot, their runes over his face
Inscribed, are the embroidery of knowledge,

And the dust of memory: a butterfly's.
"Tell me if they're out and I'll come too."

     III
So slim all of his life he could slide
Through the slot in a vegetable grater.

Now he's slipped into the grave, quite satisfied,
His body no larger than the rumpled

Spine of a good book
Around which a whole world of brown fields

And yellow whin, like his loose
Jacket with the sharp lapels

Or the monarch of his soul will fly—his life
Read over and over by the blind larvae

Off his horizontal script
Of bone. In what direction, right to left

Or vice versa, hardly matters. It is abstract,
Primitive, best summarized in the hymning

And humming of ants and sunlight on a whitewashed
Wall where I catch him now—

A sailor of the sky,
Uncle Dick, or a butterfly.

¡KINDLING!

He gave birth to a daughter. Her name was Justice. He couldn't get her out of the house quick enough. Once outside, he said she waited for him with two catapults full of stones, where her breasts should have been, where her heart should have been, and whenever he put his head out the door to see how the world was doing, she let go. Great bumps rose on his brows from the lessons she was giving him. Sunsets and stones,

they all rained softly down on him as pink as marble. On other days, as grey as gravel or his underwear. No two recriminations were alike. Whicheverway, she let him have it, and so he came to understand he was to blame for all the differences in the world, for never having let them be reconciled again with the fire, where he sat at night—in the dark—thinking up new creations with his wife, whose name is said to mean hearth.

Sometimes, he could take a poker to them both. But should he stand up to his full height, he would freeze to death in the outer space of his own heart, and would only come down on them like bits of ice and snow that melt like those eyelids of theirs, blinking at him across the endless paintings of the flames.

A WARNING ON THE SUBJECT MATTER
OF THIS POEM

"A Young Girl Stooping to Observe a Dog
Sleeping in the Shadow of the Sea"—
commentary for one of his paintings by Salvador Dali.

i

So, should we say
anything about the sea,

venture a word
on our wives
and daughters,

or put out, as usual, in our poems,
exploring for telepathic
and oracular shells

that return our calls
of chronic loneliness

with the body of a goddess
and the voice of a pearl?

i

Or will we be put out,
tossed on our eccentric

ear—cf. Van Gogh,
the castaway's

tipped into the Zuyder Zee
hoping to hear a transforming
tenderness

about setting up in a family,
already doubly
familiar
with a cousin
for crew and company.

i

We stay deaf to the horrid
hiss of our own cliché
emitted by this prophetess
in coral,

her pink
mother-of-pearl mouth, immortalised;
her soft-
centred kiss: a candy
barnacle.

i

Either way, listen to the undertow
in what she tells—this
young man, who comes rowing
to our door

is well-warned.
It is not the simple
surge of love that thralls,

it is everything else
dragged back in again
under their skin;

through them
the phrase of love

sentenced into flesh
repeatedly.

i

Take care. Once you contract
or hold these
philosophers' stones
that convert a few fond words
to everlasting treasure,

you are sunk
to the bottom of a bloodlit
sea,

awaiting a woman
or this little girl

your love became

to lift the skin of salt
water
off your back

with her greeting, as singsong
and garbled as the brine:

"Wat-er ewe dooink there,
 Daadee?"

i

Nothing moved us

more than when she moved
away and did not take us

with her.
·Myself

I felt I was
left

the dog in the painting by Dali

couchant
and sad

mimicking the rock
and shyness

tucked
in with

the hermit crab. But
octopus or oolichan

everything that sprinted by

up to some no good *busy*
ness

was just one more betrayal
by the *primum*

mobile
that makes the constant

soul
go anywhere

underwater
underground

for sorrow
or for love.

THE TRICK TO MY DAUGHTER

The first time I feared
I would never find her

she was addressing a dog,
a Führerhund,

this German Shepherd
called Nassau

(spelled
the same as the island town)

exotic, black—
displaying ivory incisors

through dense phlox
and a fence.

"Wat-er ewe dooink?"
she was asking

my question
of a dog.

As highly-sprung

as spokes
in a bicycle wheel

when they greet a wall,

his barks buckled.
"I dunno,"

his eyes relayed

a sprained
confusion in his cranium.

In all my black rages
at her ever since, it has been

the same:
"Wat-er ewe dooink?"

she queries
my query.

And everything dangerous
I can devise
to threaten or prevent her,
she reduces

to a yawn
and a chirp

like Nassau's.

Hidden
in the red throat of the beast,

a flock of song birds
opens,

a chorus
in a single note:

"Yip," I say,
trembling with the acid residue

of anger
or simply thrilled

at the skill.

1941

In the bell of the sky:
an eagle wings' slow peal.

The trees under it,
tip for tip, banked
in the earth's long dive
across the sun.

The stones have plunged down,
bombs with blank fuses
landed
in an unexploded

lump.
But they still don't frighten
the daughter cutting through
the trees
to the back stoop

for a kiss
under the lit window:

a spectacle, flashed
in the face of the house,

keeping up a protocol
at the edge of the wilderness.

BABES IN THE WOOD:
A Poster for a Christmas Pantomime

Through the blink of an open door
We can see the heart
And soul of a house in the snow

All knuckles and knees the hills
Pray in an old agony of isolation

But I have always known God was too much
To pour

Into a bucket
Or a book

Often he/she sleeps by the stoop
Counting on the heartbeats of our mongrel

Malamute to keep warm

I remember the trees on Broadway
Clothing the sidewalk all summer

And how the expensive ties in Finn's
Spent their time

As perpendicular
As saplings

Any loud design of stars
Is too dangerous a hope

To wear
In church these days

    Let nothing contaminate this trinity:
    Good taste and common sense, the modest deed

    Let all sign of excess be erased
    But what of God

    And Christ created the perfect
    Image of a self-made man?

Such blind faith

Leads
Only on the floor of the Vancouver Stock Exchange
Even on a Bear day trading venture in new gold
Or at a girlie club
After the black woman's show
When the white girl's complexion
Floats away from her body
In the floodlight

Like the skin on a basin of boiled milk

    You would eat of her body
    But are worried for a daughter

        Dear God whom we receive

        Pure as a snowflake
        On the lips

                    That same small kiss
                    Packs glaciers
          Into bed

          Wherever our children stretch
          In their slumber

          The culverts groan
                              Heaven and earth
          Are ground down by them

          And the pets in the store windows

At the theatre
Lifting like deer in the deep wood

The thighs of the pantomime Principal Boy
Make a savage leap at the heart

Late at night

Wise men and women

Never even touch

That idea of a child
They tiptoe on

Past the striped
Candy cane and sweet

Saber tooth of tigers
In the crib.

I SAW OUR LOVE: TWO HOUNDS
HOWLING AT THE LIGHT

These bright designs of dragons
hatching from the sun:

flowers & flowers & flowers,
their prettiness claws at the bank.

Gusts of larvae off the salal
settle
into mauve lagoons,
imperial purple dust—

every grain with wings:
mites', midges' or mosquitoes'?

The crocus
fattened on the delay

in the soil;
holding onto the hill;

slugs blacker than liquorice
thumbs

cut-off onto the sidewalk:
Mulattoes', Coloradoes' or Mandingoes'?

At the other end of the year
we think of the rowan

berried with blood.
On another path,

pink worms concentrate
all the pale traction

in their circular wrinkles—
twins at nose & tail;

hindsight & foresight equal—
their hello as long as their farewell;

this rising
& hanging on

in us:
like the embrace

of man & woman
that dissolves them

into vibrant spaces;
the more the blood beats

from their body
to their brain,

that pair of hounds mated
body & soul,

the more of heaven
it calls to heel.

ON THE PASSAGE OF THE GOOD
IMMIGRATION LAWYER'S DAUGHTER

He dug up stones
Until there was nothing hard
Left in their garden.

Even by the telegraph pole
On his strip of boulevard,
He heaved up a mound
Where the pocked pole
With its foot of clay
Could flower,

Its colour eclipse
Her full-grown darkness.

And all that while
He could not cut
A soft spot for his daughter
In the ground

Beside the house
He bought for her
To die in, graciously.

i

As mild as rain, her heart
Kept beating down

In the brown bog of his breast;
A mist rose

From the dishevelled plots,

Flayed by the rain
The extracted stones
Reared up, like the flanks
And stropping jaw chuck

Or the eye whites
Of wild horses
Herded into a coulee
By this émigré banshee.

Those distracted stones
Leaned all winter then,
Exhausted
Against a garage that stood
As awkward and askew

As a delinquent
On a corner, waiting
For a bus—

Finger at the lip, gum
Hardened to a tasteless
Pebble in her pocket:

A girl who loved him,
But grew difficult.

i

One night, she arrived wet-through
With it caught in her bones.

He looked at her
As distracted, then
As deranged as a photographer
In Ethiopia or El Salvador—

As if training a camera
On the disease
Could arrest it at a click
Of his anger or his fingers.

How goodness could betray.

He gave his own and found it
As lethal as the sun and rain
That kept her ill
And lovely, growing

Along with everything else
From the ground.

i

Soon, the rain
And the thirst in the earth
For a mineral objectivity
Would sift her back to sand—

Like the dregs of the long river—
Into the sea nearby, its bouldered
Ornamental causeway, so like
The cracked trail to Croag Patrick,
Lost

In the tide, idle
Where she might have walked out
With a lover, one miraculous

Evening. His rage mirrors
The old storm in the heavens
That attacks the unkind
And graven immobility
Of stone.

Poor, brittle scaffold for the stars
Her skeleton
Would never lie without collapsing
Under the weight of the inadvertent cairn
He churned up, like gobbets

Of grey buttermilk, in her memory:

A child's face in her high chair,
His queen
Waiting for the glyph of death
And every disintegration
In the weather, he swears

That struck her body—

The gale that reamed tomorrow
From the marrow—
Once he forgot to shelter
Her from terror, making
A new home, securing
A status

For others.

i

He shudders at the tiered deck,
Bamboo planted for shade
Where they sat: the air, whittled
By the pen-knife
Finery in the leaf.
Winnowed light, ghostly
On the shoulder of the afternoon.

He bends,
A pullover and rubber boots,

Slow as a slug, locked
To another rock, he will pull
The plug out of the world
Let the dead flap up

Beating like doves—out of
The twilit quiet, the dusky
Carpet of the air,

Leaving in its place
A stately tapestry of their ascent.

Or more stunning still,
A metallic flutter of springs
Through his hand

From the window blind
Each morning
As he lets go the toggled string
And looks out
At the stained deck, capsized
Over yucca and spindly bamboo.

i

If his house drifts or sinks
Into the anchorless ground,

Or seizes permanently
In a frost, for want
Of these natural heaters—

His immoderate anger
At the passing nature of things—

How much evicted stone
Will there be in his wake?

i

Enough for the beaked gargoyles
Of a cathedral, or a small chapel

Bestowed
In his labyrinth of flowers.

¡ CRUDESCENCE!

Q.   *Jimmy, what's all this about*
the origin of the faeces? And them

birds, where did they
come from
—the sky,

or the damn trees?

A.   *Out of the water and the earth*
muck that made them
like the rest of us,

you dumb cluck,

out flying after
fun and sun, all year,

with no overhead,
no air fare..

away from the big smell-
up in their nests.

A STORM IN THE BRAIN IN THE SEASON OF RAIN

The girl went outside and put her arms around
The palm tree. The boy went out and put his
Around the other side. Out of the house came
Their mother, after playing cards, looking
For the missing pair. In the first flash of
Lightning between them, it appeared to her,
They had squeezed the tree into the sky.

Through the fronds of ages, stars are dotted
And after the storm, like stalks of great grey
Celery, the withered leaves crash down off the top.

When their mother was young, she covered her
Mouth in front of their father because
She felt eating to his face was
A betrayal of her love.

Now, dining and talking openly of food
Is a shamelessness they share. The meals
She ate (which could have been air) that
Made her grow up into a woman, she recalls
Them all as one, eaten in a hurry. Who can
Say that there is not something solid
And whole as mango about getting older?
It is only when she chews the fruit
Down to the pap that the past
Clings like its string to her teeth.

The blades of tropical grass, planted one
By one with a stick, let run—
Turn tubular, thicken
And thatch over, like vine stalks that bear
A Matto Grosso of regrets.
The palm tree that her children hug, that bears
Its hairless green coconut is more fertile
Than the grass, which is cultivated for a colour

And texture under the bare feet of every
Boy and girlhood.

Who is to say the grass did not grow
These children walking over it?

In Church, she confesses to the Virgin:
There is too much mystery in this matter

To make her body
Their mother's.

JEALOUSY

There are railings round a boy's reasons
For loving the laurel, worshipping
The coats of paint on these uprights
That his brows slip through like a pew's
To the garden, where he gazes out

At the fleshy leaves, which add up
Altogether to be
As fat as his fourteen stone mother
Who is flayed
And slivered by the light on the other
Side of the bush, her body scattered
For the boy's eyes to rest on, in a different form,
The colour of soft laurel.

Athena, hunting in the beauty of the night,
Called the people on earth to compete with her
In words. When one of them bettered her
In the argument with a song of love
That broke the listener' hearts,
She flayed and hung him from a tree
For the sun to gorge on his impudence.

From dark to dawn, I hear their words
In the night sky. I am what
My father's flesh sings and argues
Through my mother's body. I have seen
The two of them blown, as wild and tossed
As a tree, my father hanging
From her—the moon and the wind slicing through

The branches—dangled and twisted,
As hairy as goat hocks,
As a man's, between her crop of pliant
Leaves.

How long till I learn that a mother bargains with the
whole world
To keep a purchase on what is hers? In the morning,
Mine stands on the veranda,

The sun beats down on her. Caravans
Of ants are headed for her toes.
She touches herself in the fat leaves,
A trader
Who knows how to do business
With the green god.

THE TOP RUNG

He looks at the shell, a womb of crude, unbroken crockery,
as though this is some round goddess who has been mislaid,
whose skin has gone dry with eczema and goose-pimpled
with the cold, like his aunt's who died a week ago. But
he can still feel her, warm and alive, tattooed in brown
and white excrement—those same limes that mortise
grit from the ground into the coarse cumulus of the egg,
and the hieroglyph of shit on his finger makes him wriggle,
like he is part of a postponed, reptilian hatching
as he collects his toll off the hen, from under its non-plus
of feathers.

The two immaculate horizons on the egg promise him
(and the brown banty) a song as lofty as a nightingale's,
but fully-deciphered, its hum spells only the same old relish
and cosy nausea in the nostrils. He should boil away the dusty
reek of his aunt, let the bubbles scour the mortared surface
and leave the flavour of the hen house—its droppings
and dawnings —trapped inside, the same as every sight,
every savour that evaporates into memory within the scrim
of his skull, the elastic of his face,

As avid as a banshee, the kettle's boiling. And who
wants him in that screech? The aunt whose hair has strayed
like straw from its thatch, whose steps falter late and early,
looking for the dead among the living: a brother back
from hugging bears and White Russians, with claw marks
on his breast; a son gone to work, or to war, or the pub
in Bangor, underage.

He can hear her call him where he's mooning
on the kitchen linoleum—a brown world cuddled
in the one hand beside a white world in the other.

Like Atlas, he weighs his two handfuls:
an older aunt who never sees the sun
and younger mother who is never out of it.
Every morning, from the dip in the road
by the river, the aunt gowls at him, her head

keeling by the milestone, where she steps out
to hail the dispatch rider in his brown leather vest
and Sun motorcycle. Like loose wings of metal
the engine is blattering, flut-fluttering down on her.
A mangled khaki rooster, or twilight's chanticleer, the rider
is not sure if his 500 cc has mown down a crone or an angel.
She croons and her bones are made of dust.
Her hot head and her open mouth
is off-circular, toward oval, keening over
the coarse carving of miles on the blay sandstone.
In his hand every morning he looks at her blood,
browned on the coarse agglomerate of one egg,
her ghost hid (like the wet
evaporated from the pot)
under the white shell of the other.

His mother watches how he taps with his spoon,
little blind man pecking at his future, his hunger
making a mathematics and a melody of loss
on the road to the coop, where heaven
has dropped its raw marker once more.

HOW I CAME ABOUT

1.

Goodness and sin, like salt and sugar
in a bowl, who can tell them apart?

Shining white as stars
poured into glass or porcelain

on our table. They lie
between us,

too close
and contradictory
for the tongue
to tell apart.

2. *Remember I told you*

I wanted to be the salt
of the earth, as pure as the driven snow,

but I learned the one
could melt away the other

and when I left for the New World,
my sister had something to tell me.

"Your father was a bastard," she said.
As if hers was not.

This wasn't meant to sting me
into staying, but to let
me taste the pillar of salt
which was my history

without needing to turn about
and stick out my tongue

at our Irish Gomorrah.

3. *Of Snow and Salt*

Grains of truth the size of tennis
balls fall from the clouds
in Saskatchewan.

There's no way around it.
If it is made of sweet
water, it will still break
the window you are looking through.

If it is bitter, it will keep
forever.

4.

Squinting along the horizon
of my history,
who should I choose for my grandsires?

Liadan, of the great
lay, and the itinerant Cuirithir—

Am I theirs or not?

Or will I just claim kinship
along with everyone else

to the great her/him,
our primogenitor,

the vanishing fruit of whose thunder
is so hard to heap
into a basket?

Or is there need, when any old
ape, primordial soup—Maggie
or Jimmy Whatyemecallem—

was enough
to get me started.

LOUD SHOUTING IN THE HALL

Does Angela still shout as much?
Ernest Douey

Your Daddy and your Mammy
were a turn. God, they used
to roar at each other.
Eddie McKee

On a bare headland in a hard wind,
like the ringing of masonry, a shriek
where their voices rose, the gulls—
turning to steel in the weak
light—descend
and rasp at the rock

like a shower of trowels,
diving at the jam
that drips red
over the edges of a piece of bread
abandoned at the cheap picnic.

At the meeting of the Atlantic water
and the Irish Sea's, a child grows
like a fish. Beneath a lost ancestry
of cliff and castle

at Dunluce,
an eel swam away
from those chimneys, twisted
like the necks of cormorants
that had been strangled, but not killed.

There they stand
where they have rotted live,
right down to their flues;
              and an eel swam away,
              an eel as long as an ell
              or as short as wrist
              to elbow: the knell
              of their ambition unravelling
              into the streams of the sea.

The wrecked walls
would rise again
were it not for the moss
that eats the mortar, the fuzz
of their affection grown over the clarity
of rock, the certainty
of stone, like a deafness.

In the middle of the city,
why did they shout so loud
and never listen? The sea
still in their ears, the rip
of mountain wind
that became the gust
of double-decker buses
that passed two feet from the door,
shaking the brown bricks
out of their housings?

And how could anyone hear,
when they clapped together
like brick on brick, the scrape
of their voices throughout
the night like trowels
in a bucket .

> *Listen,*
> *little fishes,*
> *they struggle, breast to breast,*
> *beyond any bound of understanding,*
> *bodies that discovered each*
> *other in the breach.* Even the wind

off the jet I fly home on
will not oust
the noise of that traffic
between them
in the eardrum.

Rounding the headland,
that stands at the edge of nowhere
I hear their argument as pungent as Troy and Athens's,
as full of bartering for love
and I realize they were a civilization:
two seaside towns,
two tribes that tossed
a son and daughter at each other;
their words are the offspring
of old streams in that igneous imagination.

They leapt at each other
down a back street of Belfast;
they forded the river,
for which the city is named,
and the gutters
with the fury of their opposite directions,
warred over what was theirs,
what could be ours;   *the eel*
                  of aspiration, finding a rock
                  and head of seaweed to call home,
                  wriggles in.

                  Little fish, descended from the old
                  kings and queens of the sea and earth,
peeping behind the hill,
the memory of any ascendancy
above the furrow is let
slip away, poured off
like something from a corrie or old jar
whose water got greened over
and grew foetid with pet frogs.
They shout at each other across the ruins,
looking for him in the sky and air
between the cliff top and the tide.
What scum grew over the cliff sides
that made the past so slippery,
that let him slip out of their sight?

Should they not go back
to Ballycastle?

Let whoever likes take
their heathen ease with the rest of the Irish,
she is loath to sip Guinness, or the bitter
taste of their company along with the black
flavour of her own favourite things:
blackcurrants and blackberries,
liquorice and sissy
sarsaparilla, a name
they re-brew with balls
enough for America

as root beer. Yes, the heather and the bracken
foam up her nose
as herbal and harsh as root beer.

A child drinks his fill
of black froth,
of flotsam and jetsam
from the waves under him
and the winds above
that rock his head and lift his hair
like sedge tangled with skinny strings of polyp
in the tidal race.
If she hates them,
what is it that rouses her to pick
up a clod, Ms. Fanny MaCool,
and seal the sea off to her own escape
with the same old
sod?

They went out and saw each other
at either end of the Israel Street;
they shouted as they came and went
like the nights and the days.
Did they ever speak softly?
The gulder they let out when they
wanted to come together shook loose
these boulders
with their broad backs to the water,
as loudly as the sea they heave off
like labourers where they hump
and pile up land
against a flood of taciturnity.

From the top of Israel Street to bottom
they shout across a thousand years,
louder and louder.
She says this and he hears that:
two sexes, two cantors of two religions
calling out of their clannishness
for God to vindicate
the gust and the wreckage
of their alternate storms
that tore about the gables
like children and fell
upon the sticks and stones,
the only weapons these articulate fish
had ever known, pieces of the past
to hurl at the waters
that swirl round and treat
all their roaring
as one ruin, their conversation
made of many irreconcilable stones.

YOUR SISTER CALLED ME

Your sister called me
"a Shankill Road cowboy,"
I rendered it down,
politely, and around
in my mind to "cavalier."
Both, just a manner

of speaking.
I've never been on a horse,
or handsome,
though nowadays I do
wear wide-brimmed hats.

In a cavalier, cowboy
kind of way. Yes indeed,
my twist of the repartee
was like turning suet
into lard, neither,
sobriquet a dandy:
one just offended better
than the other

until I got older
and wanted to be a cowboy
garbed
in a cavalier turn of phrase

for those Bangor women
or anyone
who'd listen—cat, dog,
albatross.

I still roam
in the up and down
of my accent,
my dialect,

like a sea bird
over seaweed humped

on a beach
and stinking after a storm,

all my talk and my politeness
like a buzzard
that cannot land until the meat
of yon matter of origin is dead.

OVERBOARD

The orange is a heavy round flower
with petals of juice under a soft, elephant skin. Dung
of sunlight reborn on the branch,
                                    how lucid the savour,
how long the memory lasts
after its trumpets erupt in the mouth;
                                    the instrument
crushed into a music on a tongue, the
colour of sun; a sea flavour
                                    that has learnt to fly
from salt into sugar, delicate as a gland
splashed through the window of the blood
into my eye that now takes in what the mouth
has eaten, for gospel.

                    Before the unbroken segments
                    of its hemispheres shone,
                    360° of horizon grown
                    under a pap of cloud.

I peel the tree into my palms,
the sea

wet as the first hands I laid on oranges
that rolled in,
broken through the bleached wood of their boxes. Escaped
their cedar compounds as they were herded overseas—
the round animals of the
Floridas, to become bellows of another world through

the storm. The gleam of Africa in the Americas
I pursued through the soft dinosaur
skin on my fingers, the glinting tusks of citrus
on my tongue, never before tasted by me or my kind,
and never again,
until after the hostilities. This convoy
of armoured fruit sailed down
over mountainsides of water
(like Hannibal and his cumbersome
engines of destruction) with fleets
of flying fortresses for the GIs. Like solid dandelions
that whole shipment
of vitamin C was blown into the water

to seed our ignorant stomachs or the ocean floor
with an orange grove. Still, I remember spearing
them in the wave, dunking, with them bobbing
around my brows like farts of warm sulphur, a schoolboy
with satchels of incense, plodding up the beach,
and as I polish and polish the gloss
and coarseness of your memory,
still I do not know whether to kiss
or eat you,

as the Sultan said,

the hunger in my eyes
and hands has been in love with you so long.

A SETTLEMENT WITH THE ANIMALS
(*in Four Clauses & 1 Codicil*)

Our tribe loved livestock to converse with,
animal or human, with no gap
between their traffic and ours
through the house into the heart of the Settlement—
a fortress made from a square of stone cottages
with through-halls.
When the animals were in, run through it,
and all the mud and shit shaken off
    (as if they were an army
    of irregulars, scuffling and racing,
    always in retreat),
when our animals were safe, then we were.

From the small front windows we could see
an enemy encroach;
from the back, watch our clumsy cattle turn,
debating the cud
while we went out to mop up the blood and rustlers.
For a house made of rocks and whitewash, in winter,
the beasts were grand heaters: those leather bellows
with wet muzzles
blew heat from the heart better than any hearth,

and cheaper.

Something of the sleeping close to them
was passed down to me
when we got a dog. Something
in the look of her: the square muzzle,
both bovine and brutal, of a beast whose tail end
could out-samba a shark's
                    when she had a rag
or a rat in her mouth,
or a golf ball,
              bitten through to its elastic bands
that would spin between her teeth—a twitter
of rubber
     squirrels, who were the only other animals
she would bark at
                    for their mockery of her.

In the forest, a nestful of disturbed hornets
was nothing in her maw, but that high laughter—
the judgement pronounced so lightly,
                              as if blown
in the fresh language of the trees
              along with the never-to-be-gotten
birds'—
was a rippling bite

from incontestable teeth.

Immediately she felt the traces of the leather lead
across her shoulders, she hauled like a horse.
Heaved, as if carts and carts
were backed up behind her, loaded with
the contents of the house
and a contentment in me that every time I took the lead
I ended up, dragged behind
where I could see how the beast
that wished for no harness
was what had pulled me to where I stood
                                                    all too often,
blinking from the road edge
                            at motorcars
before crashing across
                        into the forest
behind her nose.

Which read the leaf ends and the chemistry of information
in the wind.

        Where her nose went so did my eyes and senses,
they delved into the secrecy of lives that move
only when we stop:
                        the furtive multitude of bush deer,
brethren of rodents who mean nothing
                            to our nostrils
outside of linking them
to crumbs blue-mould-ering in cupboards, or garbage
            ripening
                    in the back lanes. Yet,
in their motion, she smelt the alpha and omega:
the sweetness of the new blood

and the old carcass together; the scent
a pelt gives off from the damp
and dirt
     that blares through the nostrils
when mixed with that sea of dissolving chemistry:
a dead animal.
              For her, it made the corroding fur
a tremolo, as pungent but appealing,
                      as traceable, as distinct say,
as the squeak in the skin of a guava
against our teeth.
            As seedy and sour, and original in its spoor
as the burnt-out rubber
            aroma
laid along each skunk track.
             Sulphurous reminder of what we are:
     the hairy,
still-wandering smoke of an eruption
over the earth,
the mobile fruit of bacteria and a volcano.

It is the stink I had forgotten of my own kind
in the byre of a house I come from.

What God once waited to be born in:
a shrine of dung and odour; winter
earth,
     with the mark of the beast,
the print of her heart
still warm within it.

Codicil

The brown
world snorts and blows like a muddled boar,
or brindle terrier that lives
in the air.

Whoever has the chore to look at the earth
passing through the skies
and open the door to our settlement
with the beast,
then shut us in for the night,
please tell this coarse-tongued and hairy
                              constellation
licking the light of morning
        onto my face,
she has no reason to fear
                        if she wakes me.
Ursa Minor, muzzling my face,
had no call to let me lie
and hibernate so long.

THE ANSWER TO ALL WANT IS THE KIWI

I can't argue with the halved
emerald green of the kiwi,

or look this iris
veined with juice

in the eye
to be eaten.

Who laid its furry egg on a bush,
invented the gooseberry again

as a Titan,
or dun cocoon about a Madonna:

her body blinking, thronged in the oval green
grotto

of her sequinned robe?
Like the Virgin of Guadeloupe,

you are laid open,
burning

under the silver spoons
on our plate. What a strange people

we are who come to worship this meal,
wanting in belief, but brought into

a new encounter, where
an emerald green blood can seal our lips shut

with glucose. All the old bitterness,
all the prickles, all that pale bald-headed

greenness has gone
into a transformation,

monster, woolly mammoth. I feel
its rampage, the stampedes

and ripe despair at all
who have gone before

into the land of plenty:
the bearded men of religion

and revolution, whose green ideas
put their head on a plate. Ramón*

who I can argue with no more
now they have dropped your brain

down a well. The sting of our last
conversation on my tongue. What

I can say to you in a kiwi
the virgin only knows or the prayers

from all mothers with the furze of their new-borns'
heads heaped on the floor of the Basilica.

How can I lay up my appreciation of the difference
in taste you took too far, scoffing

at the infinite jade marmalade
on universal toast. Fruit

I thought too gargantuan
for anyone to rant on

about until I got my teeth
into this subject of a kiwi.

December 16, 1988

THE ROUGE & THE BLACK

Nothing hurts so hard as the bite of a ladybug—
that sea shell, that red and black whelk—
that leaves a welt of disappointment

where it fixes
its vexation. That small
(whatever it was?) sun,

in a radioactive rage over its
blemishes, its black spots—ate
a molecule of my skin. The pain
appeared to come from 9 million miles away

like your look when I said "Hello"
to you, behind your sunglasses,
and you said, "Pardon?"—smiling
with your lipstick and not your lips.

That's when the twain came unstuck,
or together—the diminutive colours
of pain and beauty, their whetted
relativities dug in

between skin deep and heart-felt,
as you too nipped me with your painted
fingernails. Such a sting isn't like
the irritating, anonymous green

of nettles (that vermin
of the vegetable world) or dock. In league
with the mottled magic of mushrooms
that can murder with good looks
and beauty spots,

you two gave me the incision of your opinion
taking a snippet of my flesh
for love's lab

where, under a microscope
of disaffection,
you examine me, live sample
of consternation at the lesson
I must learn:

To have a passion for patience
and patience to wait out the smallest
passion. To be grateful that I drive
anything to bite.

That I find myself in the least part tasty
to you, my love, my sweetheart,
my little dot of rouge and black in the cosmos.

1. Digital

The toes she walked on
were intimidatingly

odd: the big ones
like scallops

marinated
in brown vinegars

and a sour
succulence

from the sandy
soil and the sun

that stings her skin

with an enduring mortality,
even as I try to immortalize

her toes
in memory:

Carnalea, Castelldefels,
Ucluelet, Cuautla, Huatulco,
Jericho.

In the shifting
sands

of time
I cling
along with those scallop

toenails
to her paddling
feet

proving that

2. **Love** is a sail and a mollusc
dressed in silk: tight, fat little twat

armoured, in its interior,
with resentment,

then, a bleached
mussel shell

on the beach,
painted blue by the sky

that turns it from life
into a new ornament
for our living room.

3. **The gods**

To them—
life is an intellectual
pursuit.

They aim

to make our futures
into histories—

Scylla
and Charybdis

while we
sail by

in the present
tense

under the tearful
stars

that fall
into infinity

from a gorgon face.

SABBATICALS

After a year and a day in Cataluña
my wife and I set sail from Barcelona
on the Chusan, a Pacific & Orient liner.
Aboard, I turned somersaults
in the small ship's pool: one push,
then flip, like a record of bleached
skin, I played over and over in the water.

On board too, we met a boy I had taught in Bangor,
son of a missionary, returning from India
with his family. He watched you, dove
for rings in the ship's contest and won,
hands down.

In the pool and on our bunk at night, I kept rolling,
rewarded with yielding constellations
of sky and water.

On the second day out, dolphins paired
with our vessel in the turquoise
tide of the Atlantic, beyond Gibraltar;
they used the ship's bow wave
to choreograph their leaps. Ensemble
and consecutively, they appeared,
and gleefully to mimic me
in my hurdles, for I was
in love and leaping
time and again between the Azores of your limbs,

that dream, more salt and moist, more porous
than the dolphin-dotted Atlantic. Thus,
the boy and I pursued our own spring-
loaded exuberance, but knew our mission
would be to return, nocturnally, to pick up
the dog collars of a lover's calling,

white rings of moonlight off the deep,
and to arc away under Pisces, intent

on touching those blue fronds
in the nomad foliage of ocean,

winning your breasts,
hands down, over and over.

COLUMBUSCADE

Columbus thought Spain
was rubbing each of her good
things into his back
to make him turn round.
He tightened the slack
on his face and deftly
turned paradox
into pun: "I shall
circle," he swore,
"and scratch her behind
with a quill, re-
shape the map
of the hemispheres."
(But History encroaches
from the rear,
perennial bugger,
and squints with hind-
sight at the begetters.)

The country was nearing
her peak. All night
her beacon-fires stood
out like nipples
on the brown sierra,
and every hand came
tense and hot
for work. "Sodom
And Gomorrah," Columbus
thought as he touched
the wooden helm.

Time laid her customary egg
and dawn, the blind albumen
spilled, dragging the sun's
yolk over the rim of a pewter sea.
Breakfast, compliments of God.

But Columbus thought
with the light
weighing heavy
as flesh upon his back,
"The Whore regurgitates
a breast over the lip
of her gown."

Now, he tests the wind's pulse
in his sail, his eyes bore
through the rising cusps
of the waves to tap
raw emptiness in the west.

Such confirmation didn't help.
It seemed right on calmer
days to crush
the sea while it breathed
like a wrinkled scrotum
under the heel of his boat.

Then slowly, like honey, his clear
intention began to granulate.
Columbus never saw
the assumption take
full shape. A part

of it tipped and tilted
among the waves, almost
swamped by cruds of foam
and yesterday's sour vapours
rising up as mist.

On the ocean's other side
breakers in milk white
uniformity crack
their white-capped knees
on the step.
The generations dressed
for first communion
on a crust of sand
in an endless procession
of teeth.

The concomitant proved
nothing. What Columbus performed
was an act of faith.
His promised world
crumbled in the trough
was dragged back like sand
in an undertow.

As he swallowed his splintered
pride, truth's grain
of salt nagged
at the dry, flaked smile
on his lip.

He turned
without hate,

without anything at all
in mind
to the glittering heap
his mouth would cling to
like a tit.

¡AND HOW IS THE WEATHER IN VANCOUVER, DARLING?¡

An Exchange in Verse
About Longitudes
And Longing
For Other Latitudes

"And how is the weather in Vancouver, darling?"

Your eyes close, and your ear feels warm on the
receiver.
You hear the heat of your resistance hiss
across the ice from Toronto to Vancouver,
where you see
a crocus droop—
long, loose purple sac—
from your sister's nostril, a liquorice
black snail bask beside a banana slug
on her tongue and leave
a slime of lies across the twelve hundred miles
of phone call between you.

Her rave—about a fantastic
star magnolia, the white claws
of whose petals paw
like a hundred
and one cats' in her flower bed—
has grown into your pique:

"How grey? You haven't said
how grey, darling?"

She tells you, "Sis, you have to learn
to love the grey blues."

Exactly what Vancouver gives you:
the grey blues. "And coming? No, Sis?

not this year," *you tell her.* "Barbados
is so much cheaper. And where
you're at, Sis, the colours
are out of synch
with my psyche . . . "

like the red roses and red blood
that blossom in those black and white,
very artsy movies.

          You unglue your ear
from the hearing part of the telephone.
The blue sky and coarse brick, underlined
with white snow and a black trim of grit,
are lucid. The head office of your heart
is here; the soul of the family rests, still
as good as ever in suits and dresses,
their creases permafrosted in.

"Though, Sis, I do wish you were here,
the flights *are* so much cheaper
to Barbados."

Your sister has stolen your lines, reversed
them as she used to do the charges.
So, where were you
before your thoughts were so rudely—no, not
interrupted—inducted,
like recruits for your sister's little putsch,
which will soon have you saying you'd rather
see her than Bridgetown, any
morning. 　　　　　　*So, where were*
you?

"And how is the weather in Vancouver, darling."

A PACIFIC STORM AFTER AN ARCTIC FRONT

Soprano or mezzo soprano?

Bloated
Light and snow in a soufflé
Sink at the first
Baton tap
Of water from a cloud.

Where did this aria of contradictions
Come from—this flabby polar paw
Turning the wet white pages,
The Sunday morning
Psalms off the sea?

From the birthplace of pumice?

From the hiss of islands
Uttered by the earth
Into the ocean,
Where the bodies of brown women
With loose, beefy arms
Shovel flotsam off a coral reef?

Their breath evaporates
Into cyclones of affection,

A sigh for the temperate forests
Of the North Americas,
Where your neighbours,
Una and Fiona, stand
With their walks bare,
Sacks of salt in their fists,
And lace the gutter with brine.

At the edges of the wilderness,
Fat and random
Flakes of snow
Are caught, softening
In the throat of the wood.

Through the cathedral city of the conifers,
What are they singing
Through these white bosoms, the branches
Bending till they break?

We support you, we support you.

Can our pure white hopes believe them
Any more,

At nine o'clock on the grey Monday
When they are left

A litter of exotic limbs and broken
Promises

In the rain?

There is no actual weather in Vancouver.
It only exists in opposition to the frigidity
or humidity of sibling cities.

There are flowers,
trees and mountains,
but the rest is made up of a loose
atmosphere, akin to incontinence.

In the mist, each imagines a mental weather,
finds it mild enough to dream, outdoors

(of flower-scented thermals
and cockatoos making sonata
of the gossip in coconut palms)

without fear
of hypothermia.

In this, it extends the jealousies
and dislocations of our country.

In December, the distance
from Toronto to Cancun
is shorter in miles
by the same amount
as it is cheaper in dollars

for airfare only.

TAKING STOCK

1.
Outside her store,
the hairdresser is flogging a tree
with her doormat.

What did it do? Not let the light in,
or lose its leaves and give access
to too much winter?

2.
The coverage is there and gone,
either way it did wrong,
and if I do,
will my love molest me
with the bristly jute one

at our basement door

once the fact and I are
driven home
that the shares I bought
in a snowboard Co.— 'Ride,
(it's called, Baby—Ride,'

I told her
like it was a chart-stopper
of lyric opportunity: the wild fling
of a song we shared)
now all turned
to 'Slide, damn it—Slide!'

3.
The aeons idle and wriggle with the rain,
its translucent measles on the windscreen,
then my face as I arrive,
enter by the basement.
and find our clothes
inside to dry again,

the legs of my pyjamas splayed
and knackered on the wooden
rack until I put them on for bed.

4.
And after? Some will live in the hills
for months between avalanches
of sunshine and snow, but my skiing season's
closed in a blink of my true love's eye

over the hill of her shoulder. Am I in, or
out—to take my chances with the foliage?

I have the sinister assurance of the trees:
I could be lost in their wiles, consumed
by a colour, or a pride of conifers,
or other boughs that prowl the avenues.

Driving under the brown dapples of their shadows
was like floating through the pelt
of a leopard. Now, can I ever cover
the debt between my love for you
and your loveliness?

In the gateway
there was a sign: the mysterious
marking of our last careless
coitus: a snail—its wriggles left,

fanned out in a glaze—
like a peacock's tail patterned
on the concrete—creating

a plumèd serpent,
love's Quetzalcoatl of slime
from your vanished god.

After some small
consideration,
you lash it

with a swill of anti-freeze
and Mr. Clean
from the blue bucket.

They made landfall in July
and when the brown
girls, cheeks
packed with berries,
shuffled
in behind the men,

they mistook
them for Tahitian,
and this long wave break,
before the mainland
and the Cascades,
for a tropical island.

They had no idea
the snow would come down
until it crouched
beneath them
and echoed the whites
of their eyes,
the way a conch
replicates the white
noise of the sea.

The uvular sound of the river
and the rain repeated their French
so faithfully that these local peoples
made a point of looking into their mouths,
once they were dead, to see
if a font opened through them
into the mountains.

Rain poured down
and rose in the shape of trees;
they knew its green squint
and prickly riches, its liquid
jewellery as elusive

and fulsome

as the wives they dreamed
of, who spoke of them
as men condemned
to fornicate with fortune.

They had been with Louis
Antoine de Bougainville
at the birthplace of Polynesia.
They looked for the outermost
landings of that race
and found their own, who came
bob-trotting down the rapids
like buckskin centaurs
in birch bark canoes.

At this tropic...
their sweat, deeper
and more delightful
to encounter

than the rain.

ANGELA RIDES A HAVANA CIGAR

(A scratch in the dark)
a shooting star (like the brilliant arc of an idea
or a fingernail) crosses (the arse of heaven),
the roof
        while she sleeps,
                        or only the one half of it: one
hemisphere—a parenthesis (of skin) that will complete
itself on the other side of the world,

her snuffling universe. Within it, her breast
touches an eternity
of fingers that tabulate
time and flesh, turning back the tides
of the Caribbean for her,
like bed sheets, twice a day. But far
from Cuba, when colder than a husband
at 12 a.m. the arid space above her
appears
    to crawl in beside her,
                        she grunts at the knees as bouldery
and hard as asteroids,
                    this unwelcome ventilation
between the sheets. These hurtling
interruptions to her dream of Cuba
                            make her kick back.

A whole hill rears up outside her window: the white, night-mare
of paradise; the horse of heaven snorting into snow,

which falls now as ordinary as oats
while the laburnum braids its yellow leaves along the trails
to Havana, counting its poisonous pods, its powerful peas
wrapped in velvet.

She murmurs into her sleep: *Cuba,*
where men fence for her honour with sugar cane,
where pens are lifted when she passes
and put to punishing the pages when she's gone—
the white linen shirts of the cane cutters, the canvas sails
of the corsairs, the needles of the mosquitoes,
who tack to and fro, seek to unsew

the fabric of the dawn: pleated, folded
like the frail white net
over her toes.

Marinated in shadow,
                    her eyes grow bigger, browner
                              than her belly in the night.
When she kisses skull and crossbones,
        it is the cupid mouth of Captain Morgan
under the beard of Fidel Castro. She tosses out
the ideologue, the pastor of sufficiency,
like the wrapper off a cigar,
like a condom.
            Let's make smoke,
                         she says to all the strangers
                                  aboard her,
while rolled in a leaf of golden slumber, capsized
in a snore. Spent—from a lifetime of daylight,
fumbling for lands and hands that overlapped her
like tobacco in the dark.

The birds are too fat to sing;
Their throats, too full of worms
To warble;
Instead, they gurgle
Or go mute. When the weather turns,
They hold their beaks up, angling
Their heads to drink nature's champagne:
The rain. And my main
Friend here at the Institution, a very
Learned friend, who has written A NATURAL
HISTORY
OF IRELAND, an expert—
He is quick to assert
That the pure silk of their silence is sheer misery
In the morning. In his inventory
BC has no proper songbird—
An orchestra without first, second or third
Violin, without clarinet or flutes.
The stringed instrument is the rain;
Our piccolo and cello: the stream
And the river. Impresarios of mountains dream
Over the talents they sustain;
They have no disputes
With the birds for concert room. Trained to plop
Down on the ground, to listen to every drop,
Robins stand on guard for the
National anthem at the end of every shower,
The pitter
Of applause for the water,
That comes slower and slower
Until uh?
Rain stops doing the job
For those choked-up, songbird SOB's.

IN THE GINGER-SPIDER TIME

In the ginger-spider time
they web the trunk of my car
and lace the rear light
in the mobile needlepoint of a doily
Homey as can be the spiders live
on the heat of my exhaust,
which flutters with transparent effluent,
like a vent in the ocean floor
blurred with plankton.
                              When I brake,
they writhe around my stoplight,
as mustard-seed small
as the blood cells boiling in my head
at you in the driveway, shovel heaped
with fresh hail that has smitten the lane
in my absence. You laugh and hold it up
as though it were ice cream for me to lap,

our last taste of living on the hill—
a spritzer of sky and ice
before we decline 200' to the tropics
of Kitsilano and a Congo of leaky condos.

I want you to see the spiders struggle
to string their ginger restrainers
across the trunk and rear end of my Volvo.
They are betrayed by an instinct
that plots the points for their voyage
in swinging caramels across a terra nova

of rust and carbon monoxide.
They cannot stay unless *we* stay put
and never lift the lid. Unless I let
them make a cave of the car
with me inside it, their Robert the Bruce.

You tell me to rest, double vested
in my own dark ages.
When the clouds clear,
the sun grows better on the water
in Kits. Either I come or you Shanghai
the spiders, garnishee the auto
and gad off for those coves
where the clouds will always lift
and sunset feed
on the horizon, like a flower.

WEST FONT

You, who own
The sunshine places,
Eat home-grown
And dried raisins. Our faces

Evade those succulent
Wrinkles
Because, for emolument,
We marinate in shadow that kills

Them. We float, a wadded flabbiness,
Like phosphor through the rain,
Ready to incandesce
In a wet white flame

Of disdain:
Water saints without name;
The liquid icons,
Which you, desiccates of Saskatchewan,
Would dip your fingers down
Into and drown.

JERICHO

(Pet rabbits were released in Jericho Park. Coyotes
came, eagles came down. Only the canniest survived
to nibble among the barbed wands of blackberry.)

Like the hawk, like the owl:

the whole axle of the sky in the search,
in the turning of the neck,

is twisted to see what comes up behind, what
gathers where we need fly

to open the eye of the weather, slay
with a sere kiss the atmosphere

between us that cleaves and leaves
its electrocuted jerking

as when a claw of complete competence

attaches the raptured
clumsiness of a rabbit

like me to you. *What do I see,*
where do I go?

The black thundercloud rolls
over a flock of black crows

and lightning strikes
the goat with fright

before them.

This is what the tempest is seeking:
carrion, to spit on

and restore
with all its fur and feather

for evermore—who has wished for other
than to put the meat they feast off

back on its
feet. You and I

who fulfil the cloven dream
of the Seraphim and see

ourselves flutter on three wings

(as good as Father, Son & Holy
Ghost) in the light of God's eye

as fluid with gravity
as the running water.

Oh, to wake as newly
as the wet red wood of Jericho

as the vulva of a mother
that lets light into the glands.

Perchless bird, the soul,
flying in from so far

with everywhere

and nowhere to land,
but you.

IRRIGATION

They say if you water trees in the late evening, it is like
pouring water up a wooden hose into the sky. Similarly,
dreams are drawn from the stuff of day and siphoned off
into a stratosphere, a reservoir of mental, muscular and
involuntary reverie that circulates in a virulent weather
of its own, a system of cloudy thoughts, of hot images,
compressed air that precipitates drop for equal drop
into the heads of others, who wake, feeling and knowing
you, a neighbour, as their familiar, the way a tree knows
the rain.

Darling, did you realize that you are those showers,
squalls of erotica that toss your neighbour to and fro,
under his twill bedspread, in the dead of night?

I might ask you and him to be faithful, but that would be
like trying to put a cork in every pore of a tree.

A votre santé! I drink the revelation, this rainwater neat.

¡OVID IN SASKATCHEWAN!

For **Alan Safarik & Dolores
Rymer***: Saskatchewan, the heart
of corn, the core of everywhere.*

*the rest of the pantheon's
taken great Caesar's side, ganged up in a pack
to load me with troubles as myriad as sand-grains
on the shore, as fish in the deep, as eggs in fish;
you'll sooner count flowers in spring on wheat-ears in
summer
apples in autumn, snowflakes in winter time
than the ills I suffered, miserably driven all over
the world* en route *to the Black Sea's left-hand shore.*

TRISTIA, Book IV, Ovid.
(Translation by Peter Green)

*Ovid Naso was banished
by Augustus Caesar, never to return to Rome.
Why has been a subject for speculation over the
centuries.
Some say he was privy to an imperial impropriety
within Caesar's family. It could never be forgiven
or allowed into the light of day.*

FIRST ECLOGUE

In the capital, I swore I would
keep them awake at night after they went to bed,
not with the mute mysteries that men and women's lips
discover in the dark, but with what Ovid had spoken
about love. Now, I slap my hand with a stick
like a schoolmaster who is his own worst pupil.

I cannot comprehend my audience.
                                              The prairie
is filled with its own amazements:
the thunders and tunnels of dusty air it can drill
into a sky as dark as granite
and as light as limestone, plumbing upward
for the core of the sun. It baffles me,
but is overall content with its own endless
circularity
like a great green fish in a bowl of air
with its mouth open, saying: 'Ah, am I not difficult
to believe?'
                    It's hard to grasp why I am here
or the braided tops of the grass that toss
in the wind, as pod-plenty as wheat, but seedier
ready to be blown further for no reason
that I can see. The herds are
culled, a muscular crop that thrived an aeon
or two for the tribes who pitched camp.
Like grass in the wind. As soon as their
sticks crossed in a new place, they blossomed
with smoke. I have an urge to lie down

in the durum that they will roll under a stone
and roll again with water to make spaghetti
and noodles, pretty pastas for the palate like my verses
were. I have a yen to hurl
my laurels out, and loosened from the ground,
let the stalks of my legs blow away completely;
the rye wheat of my words, cultivated and milled
in the capital, is already tossed out to seed
on a sea of taciturnity. I am spurned
by the women as if the mumble of wit
and compliment I bring will sour their dugs
or the dough for the bannock before they roll
it in baking soda. I stare at the brown travellers
in the grass; I marvel at how their horses roll
by me like boulders and decades after that, the
harvesters—
a factory on wheels that takes the wheat and chaff
of the limitless field into its flailing surgery—
so should I be separated from the gross matter
of my recollection. I saw a god joined to his own
daughter and believed it real, not a myth
my mind had made out of Caesar
sampling the goodness he had sired. Because
of my eyes I am forced farther and
farther away, to look harder at where I came
from and everything else I might have
seen or said.
            This is my error:
to say what I see; I have the temerity
to ask of the sun in the sky, 'Why
this interest in incest—can a fire
catch up and copulate or ever be one
again with the light it sheds?

As punishment,
the skin around my eyes is tugged into crows' feet
by the glare. I look down and I see I am
carrying nothing but the cloth I am wrapped in.
A bundle of complaints nobody could bring
to market, or is allowed to, by law. What
I think is heresy and loses me everything.

SECOND ECLOGUE

Blown by crazy ideas to the edge of civilization
into an ocean of grass and trees, I have
watched through the leaves and weeds
as the notices drift in,
like the desultory traffic of an afternoon
to take coffee at the diner in Dundurn
and tell me of commotions and promotions
among my peers. No poem or play of theirs
has changed the world or any letters of mine
the Emperor's mind. Frequently, I meet a legion
of boxcars in Saskatchewan, a hundred of them—engine
at the front and rear—clanking through the unseasonable
green of June. The brakeman of the column
will ask me, "Who are you?"
I put the same query to him in the same accented Latin.
"A parrot," he will say to the others he imagines
at his shoulder. "Perhaps you are all parrots here,"
and he will begin to giggle.
                              Never repeat a question.
Never repeat what you hear, I have told myself often,
or you will be as hated
as indigestion. *In what*
are sardines and parrots
alike? In that, after you eat
them, they repeat and repeat.

"I am either a sardine
or a parrot," I scream
at the centurion of the boxcars,

but the clanking and his belching after his lunch
out-grate anything I have to say.

What could I do for anyone
with my confessions of grass,
my wandering? Now it is the erosion,
foot by foot, of the metro-
politan that is my real measure;
the addresses I choose to forget
unmapping the streets in my head until they are
turned, curb to cornice, into an empty plain
which about covers the difference between me and the capital
I disgorge: its shoals of legs
I have lured along with me, the lips
of those Romans reciting the raw rhyme of my calumny, the hips
that turn away from me in my sleep
like bream at the cold hook
I dangle without the worm of love.

Instead of that meaty perfume,
I inhale long lines of landscape and the stinging
scent of thyme: this lingo
that blows in Gitic or Ukrainian with its
dark uvular embroidery—like the wind
in a charred tree, its leaves rewoven
to a black silk by the flames,
and all the faces I have known are charcoaled in its phrases.
The afternoon wipes away even as it lights up their features,
this time, in a broad stroke of sheet lightning. I can
no more halt these brutal tidings
          than the storms and the ides
of June crashing into the grass, leaving it

as though flattened
by flood water
after we have left off making love
in the ditches of this grassy dialect.

I write in this wide measure
and I cannot change a word.

Even if I could, I would be no less difficult to grasp
because what I have to understand is the knowledge of ants
and grasshoppers, the great colonies that
progress and organize
under my feet. *I see fourteen Romes*
razed in a day, an infinity
of citadels. I give
the forgiveness of clouds, of my
shadow to the ground. I touch
the baked clay at the edge of a pond
with my sombre thoughts, that
have no weight, which blow slowly—
bails of dark memory. Sitting
under the salt
in a cellar with the actors
and a pot of vinegared epigraphs, we
moped, hoary as gherkins, goose-
pimpled with the cold, and with distrust,
loathing each others' finer features.
                              The Caesars—
when I say they are not gods,
I am only guilty of an observation,
but I do agree their power hangs over me,
their question marks

like meathooks from the rafters. Vanity
is not serious enough a motive for anyone
but gods. Not serious, but their lackeys
wade in after me and when they lose all direction,
wait for sunset or sunrise to separate West
from East, then look again. My error
is what I see, a side of the world that does not need
the other that I came from—that business
of doing business with the people's appetite, hedging
against their needs and their greed, rutting like the nose
of a trained pig, fussing at the moss
for a truffle it doesn't dare eat,
but must keep secret, its flavour
buried until another will pay for one
with a whole field of Brussels sprouts or cabbage.

There is an animal cunning, and a tame vegetarian stupidity,
where we forget
how to count in the real arithmetic of tooth and claw.
Sending me here—
like letting a pet bitch out to play with vixens—
has mated a patience
to a cunning that cannot be let back in.
Yes, I have begun to court the fox that will suckle
the rebellion of the lapdogs. He need not be
a prophet to see I no longer love
the wolf that does nothing above
what it has to
and only organizes itself
to eat.
     The fox
is the proper entrepreneur of the (unexploited)

animal (a chicken that has flown the coop,
a duck stuck in a ditch), but in Saskatchewan
I have also come to see myself and my
cleverness as two cruel
singularities, caught by these teeth of mine
and worried like a chicken, wishing to have
my own entrails read.
                    But here I am also,
reborn in a place where in my solitariness
I appear to be my own origin. Those beyond
my hearing—parents, grandparents—
the bastard-makers, not a word from them
in this wilderness that is like green death,
where they should be walking,
discussing horses for which all of us
of the Naso family have a fine nose.

THIRD ECLOGUE

What is family history to me, but a fancy
now in Saskatchewan. I have made them up
as much as they made me. I believe
my father inherited the kingdom of his being;
so do I. Loneliness makes gods of us all,
castaways and Caesars. And love?

                          The close
clouds are full of buildings. The light inside—
a haze of starving stares that feed
on what they cannot see from the 20th
and 28th floors. The arms
and the legs of the lovers find their places
in spite of the inclement, but low-
lying weather. Making love
in a fog, anyone who wants
can be the bare bulb of flesh
that lights the room. Still,
at the end of everything I am a drain
on the public's time. They will send
a courier to check that I have garnered
nothing here from these very careful
colonists and their very civic art
which is practised like good government,
like good medicine. If I should
contract a cure from them for my dissidence,
it might remove every germ of reason
for returning to the centre
of administration and all of that recorded

universe. I have fallen in love
with the middle of nowhere, the cattle
and my privacy. The griddle of nowhere,
over which a summer turns the grass
to hay, the soil to clay as salty
and dry, as scaly white as my scalp
under the hot helmet I put on to greet the world—
a farmer of phrases posing as a foot soldier.

What am I keeping out? The mortal danger
or the awful style of the
tribes here who run around, togged out in
trousers that are too tight, or coveralls
that are too loose, as if work
were a liberation, and play some awful
kind of constipation that makes men
and women walk as if their ass
and innards were tied in a knot
of denim. Nuisances
from the exchequers come,
nosing at our pockets, their stripe
more shocking than the white that hatchets
a Nubian's face in two, turning
the pelt of its expression
(like the exclamation in the iris
of its eye) into an evil,
animal ambiguity,
but can you milk an administrator
if he butts into your business
like a goat?

FOURTH ECLOGUE

A river runs through Saskatoon.
It is a new month of the old god, Juno,
and the good wife of Jove must be gratified
by this wide waterway where children
have come to hear men and women talk
like little children too, moving in and out
of the tents at a fair, full of more wisdom
in traded fables and fancies
than the tax collectors
who can only read the one line
at the bottom, which in my case
has always added up to too much money
for what I say. Indeed, they
should tax anyone who listens to me,
the Caesar says.
                  Does my boredom
have to shut its mouth at theirs? I ask. They
are too tedious to be evil, too
repetitious for me to continue celebrating
anyway. What story of mine
could keep them from their snores
or like needles in a crochet,
their snouts out of the crotches
of other people's wives? Love,
which they bade me speak of,
was an indecency I turned into grace
too often to let me continue to sing
its praises. I made conceits
for husbands and wives, might well

have talked of olives and armadillos—
the stone at the heart of the pious,
the armour and all that ugly business
that kept a plump little twat
inviolate, as unkicked
as a coral football,
or sea urchin.
        The senators and Caesar
foresee themselves in history as
abstinent, quite
forgetting the image of their
licentiousness in the mirror
of my mouth, and so they attack me still
for impudence and a treasonous distaste for Roman
virtue.
        Is that virtue a tub
of lard? Surely, gentlemen, you
would not want to hold that up
as the best you have to offer
in your own memory. I speak
only metaphorically, of an image
self-satisfied, fed on what
has been carted in from farther and farther away,
the fields beside the capital, lying fallow,
without enough vines to fill a flagon
when the grapes are squeezed. Like the tits
of our dowagers whose legs are left swinging
round like withered stiles for some youth to leap
over again. Their husbands
all in the city, tilling nothing

and reaping only the pork bellies that men in the provinces
fatten; the horde
in the larder of their own guts grows
with no exercise to compensate;
our army serves as farmers, garners
wherever it goes whatever harvests the countrymen
haul in, over the seas of ice they cross—where
you have let me slip out of sight
into the white floes
of forgetfulness, for my want of reticence.

FIFTH ECLOGUE

All winter we move
like dirt in the snow:
a blurred print
soiled with darkness,
advancing in columns or in single cars,
our lamps on all the time
to see through this purity
I am condemned to negotiate—
the white desert of a beginning,
the new page unscrolled for me
at the edge of the townships.

But I have learned the hard way:
true Latin loyalty should lie
wherever these goods are coming from;
love is owed wherever that
abundance flourishes because it gives
and dare not ever think of itself
or for itself. These provinces I should have seen for myself,
eons ago, and now am here to thank them in person
for the bread I eat, for the lumber that builds our galleys—
these stern colonists and loving natives.

The ex-army, ex-consular staff
warned me. Once I felt those knives
held at my throat with a steady hand,
an unwavering eye, I would know what it is
like, what the legions know, what the literati
can never comprehend . . .

. . . The hatred
of the audience in the grass or at a street
corner that waits for the tramp of metered
feet? I ask. The fingers of some abused
elder at the throat, who did not like me
for making free with my muse who just
happened to look like his daughter—
as parched and thirsty as July,
eyes of pale grey in a blond head; the skin
almost beige, as baleful as veal?
A chilling thing to look into that less
than godly gaze.

SIXTH ECLOGUE

Julia, daughter of Augustus—though you fall
before him in the rampage of the year,
what is the wilderness, but a reflection
of our unimportance in an infinite space of trees,
or grasses where we cannot see or hear
each other for weeks at a time, and come
famished to encounter
even the curses of our own kind?   "I swear
this foul language of mine is what you will
miss," you told me, "enjoy it while you may."
I have cursed myself into an exile
by not thanking my lucky stars
when I let your putrid tongue
wag in my mouth.

I have grovelled over him too. Oh muse,
oh Myyrha, locked into the bark of a tree
for kissing her father too avidly. There is
a scent of insanity in your sap
that men will tap and sell on the open market
as myrrh—the incense of incest. On hints
and whispers of your sex, on rumours
of what you have done, old men
will copulate with themselves in the corner
of a hotel room, making love to what they
have made in their own minds, like
a poet in heat with his hexameters,
like me.

Let me now pay with abstinence,
let me wait here for water,
the wine of the sky, to come
from the unknown sea where it was born,
let me now feel to the full the wilderness
where I cannot hope to hail
one of my own species—for days upon end,
days made into this succession of shining
kings and queens, the true line of nature's
royalty in Saskatchewan,
where the light will crown
anyone who bares their head
when they walk outdoors. I warn you
I have never seen my like
in all my life and I am not lonely
or mad.

Why do I insist on competing with Caesar, you
ask, when I have no more power than poetry?
Precisely because I have no more, I can
muster all my forces
at any moment in my mouth. My mouth
that will be my murderer, and it
is calling, talking, cajoling; it imitates
with a tick and clack of the tongue
the grasshoppers and the slur
of a snake in a slake of mud.
It is a thing making the noise of things,
not speaking of love and trying to catch
the shape of my admiration for a woman. With nothing
to look at but these tadpoles, those ants, I have become

able to follow the patterns to and from the anthill
and know them all at once as intimately
as I know the flow of hair on my
head in the wind.
                    Gathering,
gathering, that is all it is.

Can we afford to come this far
anymore? Can I? Almost beyond
consciousness, onto the hob of the sun
that pops corn
out of the ground, and loads
the kernels explosively,
like golden
shot into its cartridges of air. Demeter
and the diameters of the Empire shake
along the tracks that run like some
drunken, schizophrenic radius
toward the outskirts of geometry,
where the trains chug, choked with grain,
but void of passengers because they have drawn
off all the people with the produce—
as if the mouths went
with the food to eat it
elsewhere.
                    August has issued a pax
to all incoming or outgoing, through the
length and breadth of every part, for service
to the whole—to black or yellow,
or the pimple-pussed like me, but is the open
passport for pouring cereal
into the bowl of civilization what has

made the Saskatchewan smile
like another nourishment?
                    The width
of the brows and the look moving
through their eyes comes between
what I was going to say
like a pause in my own thought
which leaves me blank.
Their looks erase what is in my mind.
I am sitting with my mouth as open
as the river, waiting for nothing more
than the hour to pass, the sun
to sink into my consciousness. In
their kisses on my cheek I feel
a dampness like rain watering
a stone. The coldness of my face
in spite of the sun. Their lips mark
each of these things I am forgetting
and I worry for the capital. After
all it has done to me, if it is taken
from my mind, I will
no longer know why I am here.
I will be here for the sake
of the river and its ripples.
If the city looks into its heart
as long as I look into mine, it
will lose sight of itself. Like
a pure white building in a pure white light,
the citadel will vanish without a word,
without any further word of mine required
to erase it from the page of memory.

The ducks in the ditches are swimming
in unseasonable water I am told,
the grasses float like sedge. They are
living gladly in what shouldn't be. Low hills
appear rolling like green whales on the way
to the horizon. Birds accompany
them. Do they remember where
they were flying in the winter
or is it all one green world
year round for them. Do
they bring their destination
with them? It is a colour
given off by the light that
they leave and a colour
they fly to. The
face of the sun at a certain
fullness. Like theirs,
like these people. If
it never changes, I may
live here forever. My mind
like a bird
fluttering in front of their faces
as they lean down to kiss
me, annihilating Ovid—
the loudest clap when they see me,
the kindest looks
of all from those who do not understand
a word of my best Latin.